EFFECTIVE CRIMINAL DEFENSE

Overview Of The Bail Process And Criminal Justice System In Pennsylvania

Brian Manchester, Esq.

ISBN: 978-1-941645-88-8

Designed and Published by:

Speakeasy Publications
73-03 Bell Blvd, #10
Oakland Gardens, NY 11364
www.SpeakeasyMarketingInc.com
888-225-8594

DISCLAIMER

This publication is intended to be informational only. No legal advice is being given, and no attorney-client relationship is intended to be created by reading this material. If you are facing legal issues, whether criminal or civil, seek professional legal counsel to get your questions answered.

Manchester & Associates
124 West Bishop Street
Bellefonte, PA 16823
(814) 355-5421
www.manchesterandassociates.com

TESTIMONIALS

"Brian is an excellent criminal defense lawyer. He was my lawyer in a recent DUI case. Brian not only represented me, he was able to get all charges dropped. With his profound knowledge of law, vast experience, and promptness in answering all of my tedious questions, I would highly recommend Brian for a criminal defense lawyer."

- Travis

"Finding myself arrested in Pennsylvania was no joke. Fortunately Brian was at hand. I found him quick to respond and answer all my questions. He communicated well with myself, my regular lawyer back in Colorado, and my spouse. He and his assistant quickly got me out of a jam and back on the road. I would highly recommend this attorney."

- Joe

"Brian has provided us with a sense of relief. He kept us well informed throughout the process and has been very straight forward with us throughout the process. He has kept my son out of jail and was able to acquire in home detention instead. We are very grateful and would never hesitate to call him again. Hopefully there won't be another occurrence."

- Alfred & Aliette

"Brian addressed my legal concerns, and represented me and my case with confidence. I would recommend him for related cases in the future."

- Jeff

"After the bad decision, I made the best decision. I hired Brian and after the first time we talked, I knew I found the right lawyer. He made everything very simple and was always prepared for any question I had. Best of all... Brian won my case. Couldn't ask for a better person to be my lawyer!"

- Matt

"Brian is very knowledgeable regarding DUI/DWI cases. His dedication to making sure his clients' needs are taken care of is refreshing. He definitely has the ability to defend client who are accused of driving under the influence. I will recommend Brian to everyone I know!"

- A Criminal Defense Client

"Brian is an excellent lawyer. He was able to have my 3rd offense DWI reduced to a 1st offense. I was facing up to 6 months in jail and he was able to negotiate 5 days. I would definitely recommend him to anyone needing a qualified DWI/DUI attorney. He is extremely knowledgeable and very professional."

- A Satisfied DUI Client

TABLE OF CONTENTS

AUTHOR INTRODUCTION

Attorney Brian Manchester has 16 years of experience handling cases in federal and state courts. He is the owner of Manchester & Associates. A lot of work that he does in his law firm is high end felony cases such as rape, child sexual assault, sexual

assault, drug crimes and vehicular homicide. Furthermore, he routinely handles murder cases, aggravated assault, simple assault, DUI, and large financial crimes all across the state.

Education:

- Thomas Cooley Law School, Lansing, MI, 2000 / Jurist Doctorate
- Pennsylvania State University, University Park, PA 1995 / Business Management – Economics

Training:

- Attends seminars focusing on criminal law and DUI defense throughout the country
- Educational Chairman for the Pennsylvania Association of Drunk Driving Defense Attorneys

Organizations:

- Member National College for DUI Defense
- Member National Association of Criminal Defense Lawyers
- Member Pennsylvania Bar Association
- Federal Bar for Middle and Western District of Pennsylvania
- American Chemical Society
- Society of Forensic Toxicologists
- Pennsylvania Association for Drunk Driving Defense Attorneys
- Founding Member of the Driving Under The Influence Defense Lawyers Association
- Pennsylvania Association Of Criminal Defense Lawyers

What Is Bail? How Is It Determined In Pennsylvania?

Bail is security they put on a person to ensure they appear for court and do not violate any conditions imposed. You can get in trouble if you do not show up or violate a condition.

The penalties that you receive for violating a condition or for not showing up in court are your bail gets revoked, which means your bail is withdrawn and you go directly to jail. They can also ask for forfeiture of the bail. That means they can ask for either all of the bail money back, or part of the money. It all depends on what the district attorney and court system wants to do.

It is very important not only to show up but to stay out of trouble. If you pay a bail bondsman and the bail bondsman puts up the bond and you do not appear or violate a condition, the bail can be revoked or forfeited. If the bail is forfeited, the bail bondsman pays the court the amount of the money he put up or some portion of that money. Then the bondsman will come after you or the person who secured the bail to get the money back, which could include foreclosing a property or taking whatever collateral that has been put up. The bondsman has a contractual right to do so.

How bail is determined is totally up to the magistrate who sets the bail. The bail can be determined any way the magistrate sees fit as long as they follow the law. Bail can be unsecured or up to a million plus dollars. It all depends on the magistrate's mood that day, what type of charges are filed and many other factors. There is no set amount per charge. It is totally dependent on what the magistrate wants to do.

Different Types Of Bail Available To A Criminal Defendant

There are three types of bail. Unsecured, released on your own recognizance, and secured. Unsecured bail means you sign your name and the magistrate assigns a monetary value. By signing your name, you get to go home. However, if you violate a condition or fail to show for court, they can put you in jail and then come after you for the amount of money that was set. No money needs to be paid when unsecured bail is set. Released on your own recognizance is just signing your name and walking away with no amount of money set. Secured means you have to post money to stay out of jail. If there is a violation of a condition or failure to appear in court, the government can take all or part of the money posted.

Conditions That Generally Accompany Bail In Pennsylvania

The general conditions are you have to show up in court every time. You cannot get charged with another criminal offense. You have to notify the bail agency within forty-eight hours of any change of address. You have to refrain from intimidating witnesses. The two things that get people in the most trouble on bail are getting charged again, and contacting witnesses.

Magistrates can set special conditions such as no illegal drug use, no drinking of alcohol and not appearing at certain establishments that serve alcohol. There are a lot of different conditions that he can set, but there are legal limits to them. A magistrate just can't make things up. I once saw a person who was charged with his dog biting people. So, the magistrate said he had to give the dog to the police as a condition of bail. He refused and was put in jail. That was an illegal condition. Conditions can vary, but there are some limitations on the conditions. The general conditions are, again, show up, do not get arrested, do not intimidate witnesses. If you change your address, you have to notify the court within two days.

Is Bail Available To Everyone Charged With A Crime?

Yes, except for homicide charges. The three types are either unsecured, released on your own recognizance, or secured bail.

THE BAIL/BOND PROCESS IN THE STATE OF PENNSYLVANIA

If somebody is arrested and given a monetary bail that they cannot post they are taken to jail. If the amount of the bond is something they cannot afford, people call bail bondsmen because the bail bondsmen will post a bond to get their clients out. In return, the person getting bailed out or their family members or close friend or whoever is hiring the bail bondsman pays that bail bondsman a percentage of the bond as his fee for posting a bond.

The fee that a bondsman charges is a percentage of the bond. So, it is generally between seven and ten percent. If it is a $10,000 bond, you generally pay $700 to $1000. This is his fee and it is not refundable.

Things To Know Before Contacting A Bail Bondsman

You have to know that you have collateral to cover the amount of the bond. The bail bondsman is putting up their money to get you out. In return they want security. So before you or somebody who calls on your behalf for a bond, make sure there is sufficient collateral to cover the bail amount.

Let us say if the bond is $50,000 and you have $150,000 property and you have a $70,000 of mortgage on it, you have $80,000 in equity that can be used as collateral. Some bondsmen will accept collateral less than the full amount that they are posting. It is best to have that information ready for the bondsman which will speed up the process of getting out of jail.

Can An Attorney Assist Their Client In Setting Up Bail?

An attorney can assist with setting up a bond, but generally speaking, he would refer you to a good bail agent. The paperwork is done through the bail bondsmen. A seasoned criminal defense lawyer will have established relationships with several bondsmen. The actual process is done between the person paying the bondsman and the bondsman.

Contact A Bail Bondsman After Getting Out Of Jail

It depends on the bondsmen. Some bondsmen do not care if you contact them. Some want contacted frequently. I always advise my clients if you have a court date, call the bondsman and tell them when the court date is. That shows them that you will show up and stay out of trouble. If a bondsman feels that a person is about to do something illegal or skip town. They could may go to court, get a bail piece and have the bail revoked. They have that right.

When the case is done, you or whoever posted the bond, should contact them and say the case is over. It is also best to have your attorney contact the bondsman to say the case is over. Once the case is over any lien placed on your collateral will be released. If you own a house, a bondsman will put a lien on that house until the case is over. So it is always best to tell the bondsman the case is over as soon as possible.

Benefits Of Retaining A Bail Bondsman

The benefit of a bail bondsman is they will get you out right away. A bondsman will generally go directly to the jail to get the person out. For high monetary bail, say in the $50,000 plus range, most people do not have $50,000 or even $25,000 or more in cash sitting around to get a person out. So a bondsman is the less expensive and much faster way to get out. If you want to do property bail, that can take weeks because you have to do a lien search on the property being posted, and then that has to be given to the court and then there has to be paperwork filled out. It is a very long process. A bail bondsman will get you out right away, plus it is more affordable to pay a bondsman on the high bonds than it is to come up with the cash.

Do People Get Out The Day They Post The Bail?

Usually, bondsmen will get you out the same day they are hired. Good bail bondsmen will generally meet the person at the jail or at the courthouse to do the paperwork and they get the defendant out right away. Bondsmen are very good at getting people out right away. That is why I suggest people go through them instead of sitting in a jail until property is posted, which can take a long time. The longer you are in jail the more leverage a prosecutor has on you so getting out fast is usually best.

What Do The Bail Bondsmen Generally Require As Collateral?

Property is the best collateral that you can have for bonds because the bondsman knows that the houses are not going to get up and move. They can put liens on them to secure their interests. There is a lot more protection with property bail versus personal property. Some bail bondsmen I know will take firearms, gold coins, or other things of value, but they generally want property collateral. Some bail agents on the lower value bonds will not ask for any collateral to be put up if they believe someone is not a flight risk.

Finding A Good Bail Bondsman

The best way to find a good bondsman is to first contact a good lawyer. They can always steer people to bondsmen they trust and who they know are reasonably priced. At my law firm, we have relationships with bail agents across the state and we have been able to secure lower fees for our clients in those situations because of our longstanding relationship with them. There are a lot of bail bondsmen that advertise in the yellow pages and online, but some are better and more reputable than others. All the bail agents that work with us are top-notch bail bondsmen.

At The End Of My Case, If I Have Gone With A Bail Bondsman, Do I Get Any Of My Money Back?

No. The fee you pay a bondsman is no different than the fee you pay a lawyer. You are paying a bondsman a fee for him or her to take the risk of putting up their money to get you out of jail.

Can A Bail Bondsman Help Me If I Am From Another Country?

Yes. As long as the bail bondsman can secure the collateral, he will absolutely bail out people who are not citizens of United States. The only additional requirement is he will keep your passport.

If I Am Not From Pennsylvania, Can A Bail Bondsman Still Help Me?

Yes. A reputable bail bondsman will be working for a surety company that has agents throughout the country. So let us say someone from Michigan gets in trouble in Pennsylvania and the bail agent needs to secure collateral, the agent in Michigan can do the paperwork. Then they do what is called a Transfer Bond to the agent where you are being arrested. Therefore, you can secure your release by the local agent working with an agent in the state you are a resident of.

Do I Have To Be Related To Bail Somebody Out?

No. As long as you are an adult, over eighteen, and have assets, you can bail out anyone. You do not have to be related to the person to bail them out.

What Can Someone Expect Following An Arrest In Pennsylvania?

Here is how the court process works. First thing that happens is you are arraigned. When you are arraigned, the charges are read to you. It is not guilt or innocence. The magistrate tells you what you are charged with and then they set bail. Next thing, you are given is a court date for the preliminary hearing. That is the first appearance where there is a hearing to determine if there is enough evidence for the charges to move forward. The burden of proof is much less than beyond reasonable doubt. Some people waive their preliminary hearing, which means they agree that there is enough evidence to go forward, but they still plead not guilty.

After the preliminary hearing, you go to an arraignment at the Court of Common Pleas of whatever county you have been charged in. That is the main courthouse in the county. There a judge will read the charges and ask how you plead. After that the next court appearance depends on what county you are charged in. Some counties have pre-trial conferences where they discuss the cases among the lawyers and the judges and the district attorney to determine if it is going to go to trial or will be a plea. There are some counties where you can automatically set a plea date. There are many different variations of types of hearings depending on the county, but there is generally one type of court appearance where you go before the court to say what you are going to do.

If you go to trial, there will be a jury selection. Some counties start the trial immediately after the jury is picked. In some counties you pick a jury then come back on another day for the trial. If you are convicted, there is a sentencing. If you plead guilty, there is a date to plead guilty and then you come back for sentencing. So, this process can take up to three to eight months on average, some cases go out a year or more depending on the complexity. If pretrial motions are filed, then there will be hearing for those.

Does Someone Have To See A Probation Officer Prior To The Preliminary Hearing?

Generally speaking, no, except some counties have what is called a supervised bail program. In those counties, you see a probation officer who monitors you while you are on bail. Some counties will have you wear an alcohol monitor with

GPS tracking. Some counties will just have you check in with the bail agency which is generally a probation officer. Bail agents are different than bail bondsman. Agencies work for the court. It is just another layer of monitoring.

POSSIBLE CONSEQUENCES OF A VIOLATION OF BAIL/BOND

If a violation of bail is found you can be put back into jail and also there is a possibility that some or all of your bail can be forfeited

Can A Relative Or A Friend That Helped Post Bail Get Into Trouble If Bail Is Violated?

A person who posts bail can't be charged with a crime. However, the person posting the bond is responsible to make sure the person shows up and that they stay away from getting arrested again or contacting witnesses. If the defendant gets arrested again or fails to show up, the bond can be forfeited and then the person who posted the collateral will lose their collateral even though they did nothing wrong. If bail is revoked, the defendant goes to jail but they do not take money from the person who put up the bond. The person who put up the bond is called the Surety. So if you pay a bondsman and the bondsman has to pay money for the court, the bondsman will come after whoever posted the bond to get paid back.

Impact Of A Prior Criminal Record On A Bail Proceeding

A past criminal record always comes into play. That can be used by the magistrate setting the bail to determine how much the bail should be.

How it will affect your case is all fact dependent on your prior record and the case's strengths, weaknesses, and what type of charges you are being charged with at the current time.

Communicating With A Lawyer In A Criminal Case

There are two big parts to communicate with an attorney. Always being truthful with the attorney, because the attorney needs to know everything. If you hold out things from an attorney, usually it will come out and it will come out at the wrong time and the attorney cannot do anything about it. Keeping in contact with the attorney is very important. Keep in contact as often as you need to. There is no set amount of times you need to speak to your lawyer.

Factors That Determine Whether A Criminal Case Is Trial Worthy

It depends on the facts of the case and the strengths and weaknesses of the government's case and the strengths and weaknesses of your defense. There is no simple answer to that question. That is why every case has to be worked up properly.

Voluntarily Seeking Counseling To Mitigate A Criminal Charge

It can help. It is always best to be proactive. If you have a drinking or drug problem to deal with, do something proactive to start before the court process is done. If you have an anger problem, deal with that before the court process is done because that shows the district attorney and the judge that you are trying to put your life back on the right path. District attorneys and the courts are always worrying about people getting in trouble again in the future. They want people to address their problems. By doing so, that makes it easier for them to show leniency.

I always encourage my clients to do that when it is appropriate. I have dozens and dozens of people going to rehabs, in-patient or outpatient, and counseling for all kinds of issues. Counseling is always helpful, never hurtful. Sometimes you can get credit for jail time for the time you spent in an in-patient rehab center.

Should Cost Be A Factor When Retaining An Attorney To Defend A Criminal Case?

This is simple; you get what you pay for. Criminal defense is complex. So, if you want a good attorney who is trained, has the experience, has been doing it a long time, has a good reputation with the courts, knows what they are doing, knows how to try a case, has tried cases, then you are going to pay more than someone without that experience. Furthermore, experience, all by itself, does not matter. What is the experience they have? Do they actually try cases? Do they just sign people up and plead them guilty? Are they known as a trial lawyer or a guilty plea lawyer?

Trial lawyers tend to get more favorable offers than guilty plea lawyers. When it comes to guilty plea lawyers, the district attorney knows whatever offer they give, they are going to take whereas a trial attorney will fight them. For example, just recently, I went to a jury selection for a case where they dropped the main charge right before jury selection. They were not willing to do that during the whole time the case was on going. My associate recently listed a case for trial and the next week it was dismissed by the DA. Dismissals and better pleas happen when you say you are going to trial and the government knows you will.

Can Someone Switch Their Attorney If They Feel That The Attorney Is Not Right For Them?

If you have a private attorney, you can switch if you feel the first attorney is not defending you properly. If you have a public defender and want to hire a provate attorney that can be done as well.

An Introduction To Manchester & Associates

Manchester & Associates was started in 1978 by Robert Bruce Manchester, my father. Before I went to law school, I worked for him. I then went to law school where I completed three years of law school in two and one third years by taking extra classes and going year round. I received my law license in April of 2000. As of April 2016, I have been a criminal defense lawyer for sixteen years. All I do is criminal defense in state and federal courts. I have consulted on cases out of state. A lot of the work that we do in my law firm are high end felony cases such as rape, child sexual assault, sexual assault and drug cases with a lot of drug cases being synthetic drugs like Spice, K2, bath salts, and LSD.

We also regularly handle murder cases, vehicular homicides, vehicular homicides while DUI, aggravated assault, large financial crimes. One financial crime case involved an embezzlement of over $600,000. My firm handles cases all across the state of Pennsylvania. Furthermore, we routinely handle a large number of DUIs, simple assaults, general theft crimes and drug possession crimes. We concentrate on using science as well as the psychology of decision making in defending our cases, even the non-scientific based cases. We are constantly training, learning, and reading up on the psychology of decision making, which is really crucial because you can't just know the law.

What matters is the people you are trying to convince understand you. So you have to present things in a way juries understand. That is where they study of the psychology of decision making and psychology of influence comes into play. So not only are we learning the law, keeping up with the law, plus keeping up on the relevant science involved in different types of criminal cases. We are constantly updating our knowledge. I myself go across the country multiple times a year and am a national speaker on defense topics.

That is what sets us apart, just knowing the law and being in court for sixteen years is not enough. You have to have more than that. I constantly attend many courses in relevant forensic science such as testing cocaine, heroin, morphine, synthetic marijuana etc. plus a vast amount of scientific training in the DUI field. I attended over a dozen courses on blood testing across the country. I have also taken a course on

DNA. It was a hands-on course taught by Dr. Greg Hampikian in Idaho, Dr. Greg Hampikian is the geneticist that helped get Amanda Knox out of trouble in Italy. I actually tested my own DNA in that course.

Another course I attended was taught by Terence MacCarthy. He is known as one of the best cross-examiners in the world and I have gone to his hands on three day practical course for cross-examination twice. We actually cross-examine people and he beats on us until we do it right.

What Sets Attorney Brian Manchester Apart From Other Criminal Defense Attorneys?

Most lawyers after they get their law degree just go and do enough CLEs to maintain their license. That is the bare bones minimum. If you are going to take someone's hard-earned money, the money of family members or friends who worked very hard to attain it, you must do all that you can. Just knowing the law is not enough in today's society. So I decided I am going to learn as much as I can about all aspects of criminal defense from jury selection, the law, to how to effectively try a case, how to present it to a jury, how to use visual effects, etc.

A lot of times, I know the science more than some of the analysts the government hires, so it is hard to pull stuff over on me. By knowing the science it is easier to explain it to juries so they can understand it.

I have taken over cases where the prior attorney's offer was X. I got the case, I worked it up, and I got a better offer because of the work I put into the cases. For example, in DUI cases, I have earned reduction in the punishment tier just because the government knows I will take the case to trial. Being known as a fighter and a lawyer who knows what he is doing, is better my current clients and better for my future clients who have not even been arrested yet. I believe if you are going to do something, you do it right and learn all you can. Getting twelve CLE credits plus two ethics credit a year is not nearly enough.

How Are You Able To Utilize Science To Defend Your Clients?

First, you have to know that stuff backwards and forwards. You have to know as much or more than the experts on the other side and then it is just practice, practice, practice, so you can take something complex and make it simple. The more trials you have the better you get at it. It really is that simple, plus by going to a lot of training and constantly learning from lawyers and scientists I have become a much better lawyer. So it is practical experience as well as constant learning. I have tried approximately one hundred jury and non-jury trials in my career so far.

How Often Do You Retain Expert Witnesses To Defend Your Clients?

As often as my clients can afford them. The government puts a lot of things in the courtroom calling it science and it is not, it is junk. Just look at the number of exonerations through DNA where the analyst says, "We tested DNA, it's his". Then they re-test it later and show it is not. Bite mark analysis is junk science that has been repudiated by real scientists, and thousands of people have been convicted on that. many are now being freed.

There are analysts out there who falsify data such as the one in Massachusetts who said she tested drugs for years. She never did. She lied. It would have been discovered a long time ago if the lawyers simply asked for the testing data. Lawyers allowed that to happen because they did not get educated on the science and failed to ask for the data which cannot be faked in these machines. That is malpractice.

I go out of state for training a minimum of four times a year. So far in 2016, I was in Scottsdale, Arizona in January, Key

West, Florida in February. Dallas, Texas in early May. Then Las Vegas, Nevada in late May. Plus I am scheduled to be in Las Vegas, Nevada in late November for a sexual assault seminar and to speak in San Diego, California at a metrology based science seminar in early November. My topic will be the measurand issues in federal drug statutes.

We also use experts in cases where our clients plead guilty. We use them to present reports to the court for use in mitigating their sentences. Especially in sex cases. I use experts a lot to do evaluations of my clients in sex cases to get better deals or better sentences from judges. In terms of experts, I now have one on retainer that is a full-time expert forensic scientist who will review data from my cases with no charge to my client. He is a former police officer who worked in a forensic testing lab in California testing blood and drugs as well as firearms analysis, who then became a lawyer and now he is an expert witness.

There is **NO OTHER** law firm in central Pennsylvania that has an on staff expert to look at the data from their clients' cases for no extra charge. That is built into my fee. Nobody has that.

Importance Of Having A Working Relationship With DAs, Judges And Law Enforcement

If you are respected, it makes your job easy. It is not hard to be polite. When you are polite you get more in life than you do if you are not. If people know you are competent and polite, your job is easier. Last year, I received a referral from a person who works in a courthouse in another county. I have had state police officers refer cases to me. I even had a district attorney refer a case to me. You get that by earning respect.

DISCLAIMER

This publication is intended to be informational only. No legal advice is being given, and no attorney-client relationship is intended to be created by reading this material. If you are facing legal issues, whether criminal or civil, seek professional legal counsel to get your questions answered.

Manchester & Associates
124 West Bishop Street
Bellefonte, PA 16823
(814) 355-5421
www.manchesterandassociates.com

Made in the USA
Monee, IL
05 November 2026

67386580R00024